National Trust

C000230346

Rex Whistler at Mottisfont Abbey

By Hugh and Mirabel Cecil

Rex Whistler at Mottisfont Abbey

'Mottisfont had been converted from an ancient abbey and still bore many of
its characteristics; it blended with its magically charming surroundings like some
great rock or tree. The garden might have belonged to a French chateau. Besides
a formal parterre entirely filled with heliotropes, purple and mauve, flowers for
picking were not much in evidence. Everywhere were smooth lawns intersected
by water, and tall trees gesturing with low-slung branches. Crossing the widest
stream by a bridge fenced with late roses, one entered woods full of the song
of birds and carpeted with wild flowers. The large drawing-room, scarcely used
except in the evenings, was a show-piece decorated by Rex Whistler with fanciful
and delicate frescoes and trompe l'oeils of white satin quilting, suggesting a set
for a ballet or a fairy-tale. It amazed without altogether delighting the eye'.

Frances Partridge, Everything to Lose: Diaries 1945–1960

When Rex Whistler was commissioned
to paint the drawing room at Mottisfont
Abbey in 1938 he was an outstandingly
successful artist in many different fields:
portrait painting, of people and of
their houses; stage design, for opera,
theatre and ballet; book illustration, and
humorous advertisements. Above all, he
was the supreme mural artist of his day.
Two years earlier, he had completed his
most ambitious interior, the great Dining
Room at Plas Newydd on the Isle of
Anglesey, off the coast of Wales (a house
which now belongs to the National Trust).

It was as a mural artist that Whistler
had made his name in 1927 when still a
student at the Slade School of Art, with
murals for the Tate Gallery restaurant
(now Tate Britain), on the Embankment
in London. Then only 22 years old, his
triumph at the Tate had led to further
commissions, notably at Dorneywood in
Buckinghamshire for the businessman
and philanthropist Sir Courtauld
Thomson (the house is now jointly
owned by the National Trust and the
Dorneywood Trust).

AVE·SILVAE·DORNII

Whistler's fantasy panel here shows an alluring goddess, Flora, seeming to enter the house from the garden, accompanied by a little naked Cupid.

It would almost certainly have been through mutual friends that the owners of Mottisfont, Mr and Mrs Gilbert Russell, would have known Whistler's work. Among them was Cecil Beaton, the photographer and designer, whose house in the neighbouring county of Wiltshire Rex had helped to decorate, and who was a frequent guest at the Abbey. So too were the politician Duff Cooper and his wife, Lady Diana, celebrated beauty and hostess, whose London drawing room Whistler had painted in *trompe l'oeil*.

Gilbert and Maud Russell were busy perfecting Mottisfont and its extensive estate which they had bought in a run-down condition three years previously. Both had considerable wealth: he, a relation of the Dukes of Bedford, and a soldier, had made money in the city; she, much younger than her husband, was the daughter of the rich German Jewish financier, Paul Nelke, who had made a fortune particularly in South Africa in the 1890s. The Russells lavished on their country property the best of contemporary talent. The garden designer, Norah Lindsay, created a new parterre on one side of the house and the landscape gardener Sir Geoffrey Jellicoe planted a lime-tree walk on the other. Classical statues were judiciously placed without – and Rex Whistler was summoned to decorate within.

The Abbey itself was everything that appealed to him. It was originally an Augustinian Priory, the canons characteristically building on a delectable site, in gentle countryside, with a natural spring (hence the 'font' in its name) and the river, the Test, rippling over a shallow chalk bed across the wide lawns surrounding the house. After the Dissolution of the monasteries Mottisfont went to a favourite of King Henry VIII, Lord Sandys of the Vyne. A great Tudor house was formed out of the Priory and this, in turn, was added to and remodelled in Georgian times. Thus, when Whistler went there, it had become what it remains today, 'a satisfying mixture of styles and materials that charms as much by its romantic oddity as by its classical regularity', as the *Country Life* architectural critic, Christopher Hussey, wrote.

Above Ashcombe House, Wiltshire, the much-loved home of Cecil Beaton, the photographer and designer, which Rex whistler helped him to decorate. Painted by Rex Whistler in 1936

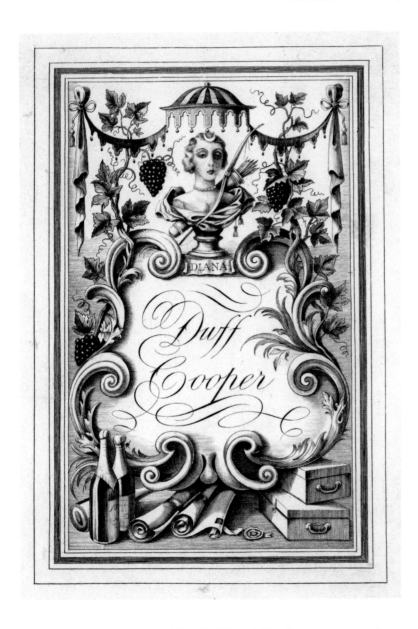

Above The exquisite book-plate commissioned in 1931 by Lady Diana Cooper, who was a good friend of Rex Whistler, is full of allusions: To Diana as goddess of the moon, and of the hunt, to her husband Duff Cooper's political career, and to the convivial friends' love of champagne and parties

Opposite:

Top
The north front of Mottisfont
and the garden's lime-tree
walk which was laid out by
Geoffrey Jellicoe in 1936

Bottom
Maud Russell

House Parties
at Mottisfont

Gilbert and Maud Russell had a large flat in London and came to Mottisfont for weekends and holidays. Here they entertained an extensive range of guests, 'writers, artists, politicians, and the ornaments of society' – writers such as Ian Fleming; musicians like the composer Lennox Berkeley and his attractive wife, Freda, the painter Ben Nicholson, the art critic Clive Bell, and, after Gilbert Russell's death, aged 71, in 1942, Maud's great love, the Russian mosaicist, Boris Anrep, and his 'Bloomsbury' friends. Among these were Ralph and Frances Partridge – the latter an energetic diarist. But however Bohemian the party, it was always well-orchestrated, as Frances Partridge would record.

The comfort was high, guests were waited on assiduously, but for Frances, somewhat more Spartan in her tastes, it could become oppressive: 'in the end the comfort itself and the ministrations of man- and maid-servants had an anaesthetizing effect', she wrote, 'But we both liked Maud very much'. Though her way of life was conventional, she herself was an original character, with something a little Oriental in her appearance and her movements. She had a great sense of humour and a low gurgling laugh. Also, though she put people at their ease and talked in a relaxed way herself, there was a hint of the dark horse about her, a sense of mystery never quite cleared up.

Gilbert, who married Maud when he was 42, in 1917, was described by a niece as 'a very humourous, non-intellectual, generous hedonist.' The Russells kept a good table and meals were cooked in the old-fashioned kitchens – very much 'below stairs'. In the autumn guests would go mushroom hunting in the woods, 'Maud was wonderfully quick at spotting chanterelles, and we ate them for dinner that night cooked in a rich cream sauce', wrote Frances.

Opposite
Watercolours by Rex,
of proposed designs for
the Drawing Room

The Painted Drawing Room

When Gilbert and Maud Russell commissioned Rex Whistler to decorate the Drawing Room, it was a newly-formed room, originally part of the entrance hall, which they made into the Drawing Room as part of their improvements to the house. Substantial and well-proportioned, it measured 46 feet long and slightly over half that, 24 feet 9 inches, across; 15 feet and 6 inches high. There are windows on two sides – a bay with three windows at one end and a pair of long windows opposite the fireplace wall.

Always sensitive to the historical context of the rooms which he painted, Whistler's imagination took a Gothic flight. Unfortunately Mrs Russell's did not follow it, although she did allow the room's architecture to be 'Gothicised': the ceiling was coved, and pilasters created in some corners. The fashionable decorating firm of Lenygon & Morant came from London to paint the walls with several layers of delicate, pale terracotta pink as a background for Whistler's designs. But Mrs Russell turned down the designs themselves.

As his brother Laurence later wrote: 'He wanted the new drawing-room to be colourful, diverse and suggestively mysterious – suggesting, say, a Middle Ages viewed by [the poet] Chatterton from Strawberry Hill', full of what Walpole, creator of that celebrated villa, termed Gothic 'gloomth'. But Mrs Russell did not want Rex's trompe-l'oeil curtains lifting onto landscapes with glimpses of distant vistas; in fact she did not want a decorative scheme that was in itself a work of art, but something more of a background. 'Really, she envisaged a superior kind of wallpaper,' Laurence concluded.

The question remains as to why, having engaged the leading mural artist of the day, capable of exquisite trompe l'oeil and whose work would have been known to her at least from photographs, if not always in reality, did Mrs Russell trammel Whistler's vision for Mottisfont?

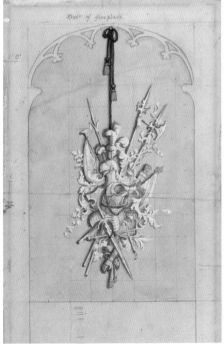

One theory is that her own aesthetic tastes were changing. A friend of Clive Bell, the art critic, she bought works by artists such as Picasso and Degas in Paris, whither she had been recently to sit to Henri Matisse. As he rarely accepted commissions of this sort, this was something of a coup. (Although she never liked the two charcoal drawings Matisse did of her and she hung them in an obscure corner of her London apartment).

Maud Russell would become the mistress of Boris Anrep, the Russian mosaicist – and his patron. No two artists could have been more different than Rex and he. The art historian Richard Shone, who, as a young man, met Maud Russell, and became a close friend of hers throughout her lengthy old age (she died in 1982) suggests that her artistic tastes inclined by this time towards Europe and the *avant-garde,* and away from Whistler's style, which did not go in that direction.

Another problem was her weekend parties. Mrs Russell was inclined to listen to the suggestions of her guests – Cecil Beaton a main culprit here – and often when Whistler returned to work on the Drawing Room after such a weekend Mrs Russell would ask him to make changes, which would alter the design of a whole, finished section, necessitating extensive rebalancing.

For the repetitive parts of the work, of which there was a great deal, his original designs having had to be abandoned, Whistler had to pay two assistants, Percy Willets and Vic Bowen. Bowen, in a poignant postscript, wrote to Laurence Whistler years afterwards, saying that he had lost money on this job, and the shortfall on his wages was to have been 'made up for later'. But there would be no 'later'.

Despite a liberal sprinkling of 'darlings' in their correspondence, Rex seems equally to have infuriated Maud Russell by the length of time the job took – he expostulated that the detail 'has to be done with great finish and flourish or it doesn't succeed'. On 30 October 1939 Conrad Russell, Gilbert's brother, wrote to Diana Cooper from Mottisfont. 'Rex, who didn't lunch with us, was painting away and said he was finishing today. Can it really be finished?' It finally was. Maud offered him £300 over the agreed fee of £1,100 on account of the painted 'ermine' pelmets and the intricate wall-lights he had designed. The agreed fee seems low in comparison with his other jobs and given the extras. Still, Rex refused her offer in the politest possible terms, blaming his own miscalculation and indolence. As Laurence Whistler remarked, 'She could now feel serene. Her conscience had been eased. Her generosity had cost her not a penny'.

Of course it was not just his differences with Mrs Russell which caused his unhappiness whilst he was working at Mottisfont in 1939. There were many other circumstances combined with his artistic frustration. He was unhappily in love with the beautiful and elusive Lady Caroline Paget, daughter of Lord and Lady Anglesey, his patrons at Plas Newydd. His father was deteriorating in mind and in body (he died the following year); as a self-employed artist, albeit a very successful one, he constantly worried about his finances; and above everything else, he was anxious about the political situation in Europe and the prospect of another world war. By mid-March, Hitler had taken over Czechoslovakia. In August, the Soviet Union and Germany, sworn enemies, cynically bought time and territory by agreeing effectively to partition Poland between their two countries. Too late, the British Prime Minister, Neville Chamberlain, gave Poland a guarantee of British assistance if the Nazis invaded. It neither deflected Hitler from attacking the Poles nor saved them when he did. On 3 September Britain declared war on Germany.

Whistler always, even in difficult times, managed to escape into his art, the fruit of his imagination and his keen eye – as would be seen in the war years to come – but at Mottisfont his inspiration had been blunted and his spirit became demoralised. Although he felt that his compromised decorative scheme diminished what he had envisaged, the result which we see today belies his gloom. The Drawing Room at Mottisfont is a wonderful exercise in the muralist's art, and in *trompe l'oeil*, albeit in a more muted colour scheme and with more simplified decoration than he had intended. As with all his murals, it answers and enhances its architectural context, evoking the Gothic aspects of the Abbey. While not as colourfully flamboyant and ambitiously inventive as Plas Newydd, nevertheless the whole has a harmonious coherence and subtlety which is particularly attractive. Architecturally, the Gothic elements of the room are created with the lightest touch – the ceiling coving, the tracery, the cornice, the pilasters twined about with delicate leaves.

Opposite
Lady Caroline Paget was the love of Rex Whistler's life and he painted her frequently. The daughter of the Marquis and Marchioness of Anglesey, owners of Plas Newydd, Anglesey, she never reciprocated the artist's love and he was often tormented by her volatility

A coat of arms rises in a riotous crescendo above the entrance doors and they are flanked by trophies of Crusader and Saracen weapons. As well as trophies of war, other elaborately decorated panels have emblems of priest-craft, art, music, fishing and hunting.

All of these are in grisaille on the muted earthy-pink background – in fact the 'shadows' are in various tones of magenta. While the whole seems at first sight subdued in tone, this only serves to emphasise the highlight of the decoration – the smoking urn which bursts from its *trompe l'oeil* niche into the room like a sudden fanfare. The pale smoke from the urn seems about to pervade the room; it has been described as billowing incense, but, from our 21st-century perspective, it seems more like a portent of the conflict about to erupt from Germany to engulf the globe. Arranged about its base are symbols of peace and civilisation – music, books, nature, romance, all soon to be under threat – and it carries the proud motto in Latin painted as if incised in the stone: 'Great is the truth and it will prevail' – as Whistler felt it would against the Nazis in the fight to come.

He placed the urn in its niche exactly opposite the fireplace, itself *faux marbre*, created by him – and it is reflected in the (genuine) 18th-century Chinese Rococo mirror bought by Mrs Russell from Wardour Castle in Wiltshire. When the fire glowed in the hearth, and the smoke billowed mysteriously, it must have created a magical impression floating across the mirror's silvered surface.

It is said that he painted the – unplanned – urn when Mrs Russell was away and that she had not the heart to ask him to alter it, given his enthusiasm for it. She also allowed his other major introduction of colour in the room – the magnificent 'ermine-trimmed' velvet curtains with elaborate carved pelmets, also trimmed with 'ermine'. Some find these too theatrical a backdrop, for of course Whistler intended them to complement his original, more flamboyant scheme. But they provided emphatic dark punctuation points in contrast with the delicate light-coloured paintwork. From the ceiling a brooding sun looks down upon the room.

MAGNA·EST·VERITAS·
ET·PRÆVALEBIT·

Biographically, rather than aesthetically, the most telling detail of the whole is all but invisible from below – and indeed it was not discovered until years later. High up on the cornice Whistler painted a tiny paint pot with a little brush in it and beside it the inscription:

'I was painting this Ermine curtain when Britain declared war on the Nazi tyrants. Sunday September 3rd 1939. R.W.'

Whistler was determined to join up and fight for his country and eventually, in May of the following year, he obtained a commission as an officer in the Welsh Guards. To this day the question remains as to why so accomplished and successful an artist was not offered a position as an official war artist. This has never been satisfactorily explained and perhaps never will be. Nevertheless, as the years of his army training wore on, Whistler emerged as an unofficial war artist and his output between 1940 and 1944 is among the finest war art of the period. Like his art in peacetime, it ranged from portraiture to stage design, and book illustrations and cartoons. But not murals. Mottisfont Abbey was his last commission in that medium.

Whistler became a tank commander and embarked for France in the summer of 1944. On 18 July the Guards Armoured Division went into action, the British objective being to take the town of Caen and end the Allied stalemate in that part of Normandy. In this, the largest tank battle the British Army had ever fought, Whistler was among the first casualties. He was blown up by a mortar bomb and killed instantly in the first day of action, a few weeks after his 39th birthday. He is buried in a military cemetery in Northern France.

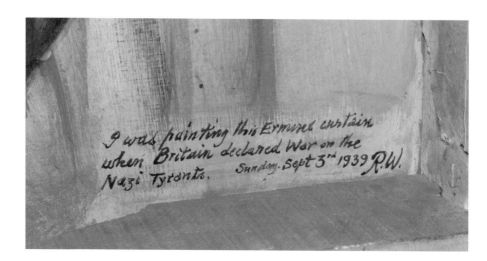

Below and opposite below
High up on the *trompe l'oeil* in the Drawing Room,
Rex painted this inscription and next to it a
miniature paint pot, with a brush still in it, and a
box of matches, indicating that he would return
to finish the final details of the room, such as the
furniture designs – he never did

Below
Rex: self-portrait in uniform painted in May 1940

Opposite
Lt Rex Whistler in uniform of the Welsh Guards, c. 1943

© The National Trust 2015
Reprinted 2016
Registered Charity no: 205846
ISBN: 978-0-70780-430-9

Acknowledgements
The National Trust gratefully acknowledges a generous bequest from the late Mr and Mrs Kenneth Levy that has supported the cost of preparing this book.

Authors: Hugh and Mirabel Cecil

Edited by: Claire Forbes
Designed by: Level Partnership

Illustrations: Authors' Collection: pp.12 (top), 22; Council of the National Army Museum, London p.23; Private Collections: pp.6, 7; National Trust: pp.15, 20; National Trust Images: Jo Cornish p.3; Andreas von Einsiedel front cover, pp.1, 12 (bottom), 16–17, 19; John Hammond pp.4, 10 (all); Robert Morris inside front cover; Michael Proctor back cover pp.9 (bottom); Stephen Robson p.9 (top).

Bibliography
CECIL, Hugh and Mirabel, *In Search of Rex Whistler: His life & work,* Francis Lincoln, 2012
CECIL, Hugh and Mirabel, *Rex Whistler's Wessex,* Salisbury and South Wiltshire Museum, 2013
BLAKISTON, Georgiana, *Letters of Conrad Russell, 1897–1947,* John Murray, 1987
PARTRIDGE, Frances, *Everything to Lose Diaries, 1945–60,* Victor Gollancz, 1985
WHISTLER, Laurence, *The Laughter and the Urn: the Life of Rex Whistler,* Weidenfeld & Nicolson, 1985
WHISTLER, Laurence with FULLER, Ronald, *The Work of Rex Whistler, (Catalogue Raisonné),* Batsford, 1960
OLIVIER, Edith, *Journals 1924–48,* Ed. Middelboe, Penelope, Weidenfeld & Nicolson, 1989